Poetry in Motion

Poetry in Motion

by Carolyn Luger Vermes

ARPress

ILLUMINATING IDEAS.
EMPOWERING VOICES

ARPress
45 Dan Road Suite 5
Canton MA 02021

Hotline: 1(888) 821-0229
Fax: 1(508) 545-7580

Ordering Information:
Quantity sales. Special discounts are available on quantity purchases by corporations, associations, and others. For details, contact the publisher at the address above.

Printed in the United States of America.

ISBN-13:   Softcover   979-8-89356-467-9
           eBook   979-8-89356-466-2
           Hardcover   979-8-89356-468-6

Library of Congress Control Number: 2024904597

CONTENTS

RELATIONSHIPS

REFLECTIONS: PHILOSOPHICAL

REFLECTIONS: SPIRITUAL

TRIBUTE

Poetry is spoken,
Lyrics are sung.
They're one and the same,
With the music gone.

PERSONALITIES

LIMERICK

A man once confessed to the crime
Of using a line that was mine.
My head could forgive him,
But my heart wouldn't give in.
"To err is human" you swine!

THE WAY WE EAT

The eating habits of our times leave much to be desired,
For we eat what we see advertised on TV instead of what is required.
So the body complains, with its aches and its pains
And there isn't any question
That the figure grows into tighter clothes
And we suffer from indigestion!

But, it's never too late, whatever the date, to follow good nutrition.
If we are what we eat, from our head to our feet,
That accounts for our condition.
All it takes is a try, to bid inches goodbye.
Pounds off wisely is what is suggested.
Live your body the best--the right food, work and rest,
And your efforts will be well invested!

A MODERN CINDERELLA

The clock struck twelve, and off she flew
So hastily she barely knew
The golden clasp was off her shoe.

And so it is, with ladies fair
Who don't take care of what they wear.
They lose a little, here and there.

THE UNATTAINABLE

At her door there is congestion.
All her suitors just arrived
Vying for her rare affection
With some marriage plan contrived.
But she falters near their net.
Is there not one better yet?

One by one, they come and go.
Still, no gentleman is taken.
Perfect love for ever so
She pursues with pride unshaken
Owing no one any debt.
Is there not one better yet?

Comes the prince she's so long sought.
All the world turns out to see
His build, from perfect atoms wrought,
His handsome physiognomie.
But now she suffers from regret,
For he is seeking one better yet!

CLEANING UP THE CLUTTER

Cleaning up the clutter . . .
Does it really matter?
Things don't seem to get in my way.

People try to change me
They try to rearrange me.
After that, they've nothing to say.

    (So what if there is no room
    On a table all strewn
    With things you wouldn't want to give away?!!)

Cleaning up the clutter . . .
Does it really matter?
I know where to find everything.

The mail is on the counter
The books are on the sofa
The music's on the piano, where I sing.

(So what if you can't sit down
If you're in a long gown
Without messin' up your whole thing?!!)

SWEEP, DUST, CLEAN WE MUST!
UNPOLLUTE THE ATMOSPHERE!
"Ding, dong" --SOMEONE'S COME!
I CAN'T HAVE THEM BREATHE THIS AIR!

Cleaning up the clutter . . .
The former and the latter.
Friends will say they really don't care.
Though I don't believe them,
How can I deceive them?
How can I pretend things aren't here?

(For unexpected visits
I hide in the closet
And I wait until they.... disappear.)

STAR-GAZIN' MAN

I learned the difference between "planet" and "star"
    When I was just a boy.
    I didn't care to tinker with an old car.
    Grinding lenses gave me joy.
    And later on, while other fellas had dates,
    I handled only photographic plates.
    You can't imagine how low someone rates
    When he's a lonesome, star-gazin' man.

    I took a girl out for a walk one night,
    And we gazed up at the stars.
    It just so happened that the time was right
    For viewing the planet Mars!
    I rushed right home to get my tripod and 'scope,
    Leavin' the girl alone, just like a big dope.
    When I returned, I saw there wasn't much hope
    For this lonesome, star-gazin' man.

        An old star dyin' is somethin' to see.
        It's worthy of notation.
        The birth of new ones in our galaxy
        Is cause for celebration!

So now you know why girls don't flock to me.
I'm a bachelor to this day.

Though I'm good-lookin', I'm no jock, you see;
It was meant to be that way.
But if someday a sweet girl catches my eye
And holds it long enough away from the sky,
Well, then I'll have to teach her how to get by
With this lonesome--- but—I've grown some---
star-gazin' man!

MAMA'S MOVIN' FURNITURE, AGAIN

Mama's movin' furniture again—
Papa must've said she couldn't squeeze another thing in!
Now, after they have their fight,
She could be movin' things all night!
Mama's movin' furniture again.

Mama's cleanin' up the house again—
Papa's been droppin' his socks on the floor, again.
Now, after they have their fight,
She could be cleanin' up all night!
Mama's cleanin' up the house again.

   (a whistling musical interlude)

Mama's dressed up oh-so-purty tonight.
Everything between them seems to be all right.
Now there ain't no such thing as 'no strife'—
But give a man a happy wife,
And he'll be well-off the rest of his long life.
You betcha, he'll be well-off the rest of his long life!

I LOST MY HEART, AGAIN

(The Tennis Match)

He wore a suit and tie
> I wore enough to cover.
> I didn't see a lover in him then.
> He flashed a friendly smile
> That took my breath completely.
> I tried to act discreetly,
> But that's when
> I lost my heart, again.
>
> He said his name was Jim.
> He asked if I played tennis.
> "If that includes beginners, count me in!"
> He smiled and asked my name.
> He said he'd play me doubles.
> I thought of my past troubles.
> Why begin?
> I lost my heart, again.
>
> I played a losing game.
> My girlfriend was in clover.
> Whenever she bent over, he would grin.
> I saw her scoring points.
> I watched the balls he served her
> And how his looks unnerved her.
> (Count to ten!)

I lost my heart, again.

He asked me out that night.
I started feelin' lucky.
The road had been so rocky up 'til then.
I swallowed all his lies.
I had the need to hold him.
(I knew I should've told him: Goodbye, Jim!)
I lost my heart, again.
I lost my heart, again.
I LOST MY HEART, AGAIN!!!

A "KISS ME KATE" REVIEW

In the "battle of the sexes"
There is room for fun and laughter
If one minute you're pursuing
And the next you're being sought after.

Imagine what befalls him
When Petruchio tries to mate
A woman others call a "shrew."
To him, she's wealthy "Kate."

What makes the show amusing
Is that Fred and Lilly, too,
Were really mated once—offstage—
"Male chauvenist" and "shrew."

Just add Cole Porter's music
To the verbal sparks that fly,
And you won't protest what is real, yet in jest,
Or admit they could be: you and I!

BOY WONDER

Need some help with fitness?
Don't just sit around and pout!
See Tim—he'll 'curl' and 'press' you
'Til the fat works its way out.

Once a chubby baby,
Then a lean and mean young man,
He worked with weights, which got him dates.
(He looks great with a tan!)

So, if you have a boyfriend
Who needs a new physique,
Just send him to "Boy Wonder"—
You won't recognize your "geek!"

THE "RAFFLE LADY"

Here's a portrait of a lady who could host a large affair
Replete with every nicety, with mother's homey flair.
But she'd rather feed the stranger who lives in poverty
And, though she likes to cook, a career she forsook to be what she be:

Chorus:

> She's the "Raffle Lady" and she brings in revenue.
> If you should stop to chat with her,
> she could start you selling, too!
> She's the "Raffle Lady," and it's all for a good cause.
> She works for satisfaction, and not the applause.

She's been officer and president—she's something every year.
She does her job with dignity, without one frazzled hair!
She's made selling raffle tickets a top priority,
And it always appears we've enough volunteers—
For she does the work of three!

(Chorus)

Now her children are all grown up;
But even when they were small,
She shlepped them to the bungalows when she would make her calls.
Yes, and even in the hotels where they didn't know her name
She was known as the "Raffle Lady"—her claim to fame!

(Chorus)

Now she spends time with the handicapped and gives the poor
  good clothes.
She works at Bingo every week and still smells like a rose!
Though she talks to many people, she keeps their secrets well.
You'd never call her "hustler," but BOY, CAN SHE SELL!

Chorus:

  She's the "raffle Lady" and she brings in revenue.
  If you should stop to chat with her,
  she could start you selling, too.
  She's the "Raffle Lady," and it's all for a good cause.
  She works for satisfaction, and there's no applause.

SHEILA

Sheila? She'll be your sun on a cloudy day.
Sheila could make a hermit come out and play!

Just when your heart is in traction
From an affair that went bad,
You'll find yourself right back in action
With the best challenge you've ever had.

That's Sheila! She'll want to phone you ten times a day.
Love her, and she will know everything's OK.
But no man could ever confine her.
She'll never do as you say.
I wonder what Sheila's planning today . . .

(Musical Repeat)

Sheila? You're never certain just what she'll do.
Steal her, and you will find she has stolen you!
She'll win your heart in a minute
But, then, you'll never be free.

You've met her;
you'd better know Sheila is me.
(or)
Forget her;
you'd better leave Sheila for me.

NOSTALGIA

THE ANNIVERSARY DANCE OF MOM AND DAD

If you're in the mood, I'd like to samba
As we used to do, so long ago.
Have them play a tango, waltz or rhumba—
Any of the tunes that we loved so.

(She:)   **If I put my hand upon your shoulder**
(He:)   If you put your hand upon my shoulder
We could re-create those moments now.
Never mind that time has made us older—
We could show the younger dancers how!

(Musical interlude to a tango beat)

Think about how long we've loved each other,
You and I—in sunshine and in rain.
And, for us, there's never been another.
When I dance with you, it's like champagne.

(Tango repeat, changes to waltz)

I can see your eyes begin to glisten
As we waltz beneath the chandeliers,
And we dream the future as we listen
To the music of the passing years.
      (Waltz interlude repeat)

Welcome to the 'good old days,' my dear!

Carolyn Luger Vermes

FORTY YEARS TOGETHER

Forty years together—
What a time it's been!
If you ask me whether
I'd do it all again,
I can only tell you
What you've known for years—
You're the 'apple of my eye'
Through laughter and through tears.

> Refrain: So hold me close.
> The best is yet to be.
> Let's make a toast
> To you and me, our unity.

Forty years together—
How the time has flown!
Can't believe our children
Are living on their own.
Now's the time to tell them
What they've meant to us:
Although you both were rebels,
You still were worth the fuss!

> Refrain: So hold me close.
> The best is yet to be.
> Let's make a toast
> To you and me, eternity.

Forty years together—
We've been through it all,
Meeting every challenge
By trying to stand tall.
If they ask our secret,
We would have to say:
Help each other reach your goals—
And don't forget to pray!

       Then hold him (her) close.
       The best is yet to be,
       And soon you'll boast
       Of a fortieth anniversary!

(Written for Miggie and Dick)

REMEMBER WHEN?

REMEMBER THE GOOD TIMES WE USED TO
HAVE? HERE'S TO THE OLD DAYS! CHEERS TO THE
OLD WAYS.
WE USED TO SING THEN; WE USED TO LAUGH.
THOSE DAYS WERE OURS—REMEMBER WHEN?

Remember people dancing in the streets?
We watched by lamplight, while munching on our treats.
The war was over, but we hardly knew

What that could mean to me and you.
(Chorus)

Remember sidewalk marble games we played?
The corner candy store, the stamps we used to trade?
A double malted is what we always got.
We used to share it—
Those days we shared a lot!

(Chorus)

Remember summers? Our folks drove us away
To where the air was fresh and grass turned into hay.
Along the roadside, berry bushes grew.
We chased the butterflies and wished we could fly, too.
(Chorus)

Remember when stickball and stoopball were the games,
And girls jumped rope while rhyming female names?
We sold our comic books to buy sunflower seeds.

We went to movies to satisfy our needs.

(Chorus)

Remember when we moved? It was a sign
Our life was changing; we left our past behind.
But, now and then, although I'm living high,
I reminisce about those days gone by . . .

REMEMBER THE GOOD TIMES WE USED TO HAVE?
HERE'S TO THE OLD DAYS! CHEERS TO THE OLD WAYS!
WE USED TO SING THEN; WE USED TO LAUGH.
THOSE DAYS WERE OURS—REMEMBER WHEN?

CITY MEMORIES

Winter isn't winter as I knew it long ago,
With the ice floes in the gutter, riding rivers to or fro,
Under autos huddled closely in a never-ending line
And the falling snow obscured by walls that hastened its decline.

An empty lot, around the block, was all a kid would need
To ride his sled on snowy rocks and dream of some brave deed.
And just across, a view of home—Aunt Clara's fire escape,
A loving memory to be played and stored, like videotape.

So, as you see, my heart was there for then we did not know
That there would be a better place to frolick in the snow.
But, just as trees and open air are foreign to the city,
So, too, would be, in retrospect, feelings of self- pity.

I DREAM THAT I AM YOUNG, AGAIN

White hair is nice, they tell me.
The lines on my face are not deep;
But during the day, while younger folks play,
I catch up on my sleep.

    I dream that I am young again,
    Enjoying carefree days—
    Those childhood games of Spring,
    The laughter, echoing!
    The force of love is still quite strong.
    I still can laugh and cry.
    I dream that I am young.
    They say I am. Am I?

I used to care for others.
Work came so easily.
Now, must I rely on others
To take care of me?

    I dream that I am young again,
    Enjoying carefree days.
    Those starlit summer nights!
    Enchanting sounds and sights.
    The force of love is still quite strong.
    I still can laugh and cry.
    I dream that I am young.
    They say I am. Am I?

ROMANCE

POETRY IN MOTION

(A Gentle Rap Fantasy)

Hey! lady, lady
Walkin' down the street
To a hip hop beat.
Watchin' you's a treat.
If you wanna be discreet
And just pass me by
And not catch my eye,
Then we won't be gal and guy—
Just pie in the sky.
But you're gonna hear me sigh
'Cause my dream is on the fly—
No hello and no goodbye
From my 'poetry in motion.'

Hey! lady, lady
If I thought you'd still be there,
I'd buy a flower for your hair—
The kind whose fragrance you would wear
To show I'm someone who could care.
You'd either turn around and glare
To show annoyance at my stare.
Or, as if my mind were read,
No words would need be said.
Or, we'd meet again somewhere,
A déjà vu without a snare.
A wholesome bonding in mid-air
With my 'poetry in motion.'

ISLAND FANTASY

(Loving You)

Loving you is like a rhapsody . . .
With an undulating melody.
While the waves caress the shore,
I lie on the sand and dream some more about you . . .

Summer night . . .
Holding hands beneath a neon light . . .
Fantasy . . .
Seems to turn into reality.

Waiting for the Latin beat to start . . .
I can feel the throbbing of your heart.
When you press your lips to mine,
You send shivers racing down my spine . . .
It's thrilling!

As we sway . . .
All the worlds I've known seem far away . . .
Hold me fast . . .
Just as if this evening were the last.

When the sun illuminates the sky . . .
It reveals two lovers—you and I
Bound by some unspoken words, for eternity.
Loving you has been my destiny.

LOVE HAS GOT ME DOWN

(A "torch song")

Love has got me down.
I'll never recover moments a lover only knows.
Yes, I drank it in—the wine with the bitters—
The joys with the woes.

Love has got me down.
I really can't help just thinking of how it might have been.
But, deep in my heart, I knew he was wrong for me.
How could I win?

    Love has got me down; I'm trying to fight it;
    But, sometimes at night, it gets so bad
    That my pillow gets wet from crying my eyes out.
    He's all that I had.

Love has got me down.
No use in regretting; there's no forgetting, anyhow.
Friend, I'm telling you I don't know what to do.
Oh, I wish I didn't need him now . . .
How I wish I didn't need him now!

WHAT I NEED

With the raindrops coming down,
I feel peaceful and content when you're around,
And the warmth of your caress
Is what I need for happiness.

Just the open way you smile
Can transfix me so I can't think for a while.
All the beauty eyes can hold
I see in yours, so green and gold.

If you promise to stay near,
I will show you how I care.
I cannot bear to let you go . . .

With the snowflakes coming down,
I feel peaceful and content when you're around,
And the warmth of your caress
Is what I need for happiness.

But when darkness starts to fall,
It's your footsteps down the hall
That remind me I'm alone, and we're not one.
If I cannot have your love, then I'll have none.

WHEN YOU GO

All your possessions take with you when you go.
Nothing of yours would bring me pleasure.
Just leave the memories of love that we knew,
Of things that we liked to do together.

All of those moments of happiness with you
Might count to others as a lifetime,
So, why waste our tears? I thank you for those years.
The rest you may take with you, when you go.

Oh! The truth is coming on so fast
That I can hardly catch my breath!
Oh! They told me love could never last.
If that is so, then now I know
That it is not a matter of life and death.

Nothing is ever the way it used to be.
Some things must change your way of living.
So, if you take it on, before the chance is gone,
Please spare me any pity, when you go.

HERE IS MY LOVE

(My Love Is A Song)

Here is my love . . .
The sounds that you hear . . .
The music I make . . .
Whenever you're near.
Here is my song . . .
In Cole Porter style . . .
I think you will find it somewhat inclined
To tease and beguile.
Straight from my heart . . .
I meant it to be . . .
Sweet, like a truffle . . .
And deep, like the sea.

>Though beautiful songs have been written,
>None of them, somehow, would do.
>So, here's my song . . .
>Written only for you.

>(Instrumental repeat)

Why did I wait . . .
Even this long . . .
To say to the world
That my love is a song?
I guess it's because, to most people,
It might sound too good to be true.
Let them note it—
Let them quote it!
I've devoted my whole song to you!

I'M SORRY

I'm sorry . . .
That I made you cry.
You're too much a part of me
To let our love just die.

Yes, I know, you rarely
Gave me cause to complain.
I took you for granted
And caused you so much pain.

Remember the day you went away
And I went out looking for you?
I'll never forget—your face was so wet—
Then I knew . . .

That I was sorry
That I let you down.
Things will be different now.
I've changed—the 'villain' has turned 'clown.'

I will make you happy
If you tell me how.
It's not fair to judge the past
And not consider now.

I'll never rely on some other guy
Who hands me a drink and a "line."
I want you to care.
As long as you're there, I'll be fine

I'm sorry.
You must know that's true.
Of all the men I've known,
The one I'd choose is you.

I will never hurt you again—
It would hurt me more.
Let's get back together—
It won't be like before.

I CAN HARDLY WAIT TO BE WITH YOU, AGAIN

Let me tell you how it's been—
It's been delightful!
This has been an evening I won't soon forget.
Let's see each other more often.
I'd like that very much.
I feel those rough edges soften
Under your gentle touch.

We've been standing here too long—
You should be going.
You may call me in the morning after ten.
Why do I feel you belong here?
You turn to go—and, then,
I can hardly wait to be with you, again.

(Musical repeat)

We've been standing here too long—
You should be going.
Don't forget to call me—sometime after ten.
Why do I feel it so strong, dear?
You turn to go—that's when
I start thinking how it's been.
Can't you see the state I'm in?
I can hardly wait to be with you, again.

Carolyn Luger Vermes

PINCH ME NOW TO SEE IF I AM DREAMING

She: He drops me at the station
With my heart in palpitation.
I'm going back to where I started from.
After years of being married,
Suddenly I'm starting over,
Fearing all the changes yet to come.

I board the train, my face unpainted,
Feeling like I should've fainted;
But, instead, I sink into a seat.
You speak to me across the aisle,
A stranger with a tender smile.
"Would you like a drink or bite to eat?" So,

Refrain: Pinch me now to see if I am dreaming.
Now, at last, my life will have new meaning.
Goodbye anger! Goodbye pain!
All because I took that lucky seat on the train . . .

She: Life's no bed of roses
When two partners have their poses
And some things you don't share 'til it's too late.
Then comes the explosion
And you're falling in slow motion.
Things you loved you now begin to hate.
I used to be pretending
That there'd be a happy ending
And the only way to live was day to day.

It's hard to face a sorrow
So you leave it for tomorrow,
Hoping it will somehow go away. So,

(Refrain)

He: Before you came, I wasn't living.
She was taking, I was giving.
Hardly what you'd call a compromise.
She abused our only daughter.
No one's temper could be shorter—
Something that she failed to realize.

I had to come to some decision—
Life is subject to revision.
I had more than paid for my mistakes.
Now my heart is free to choose—
You're worth the gamble, win or lose.
What do they say? 'That's life, those are the breaks.' So,

(Refrain)

He & She: (Together)

With an old life ending . . .
There's a new life just beginning . . .
But it's hard to keep your footing, just the same.
Memories will follow you
And make it hard to follow through.
They'll say you don't know how to play the game. So,
Pinch me now to see if I am dreaming.
Now, at last, my life will have new meaning.
Goodbye anger! Goodbye pain!
All because I took that lucky seat on the train . . . . ..

RELATIONSHIPS

TO MOM

Music there will always be
So sing again youth's melody
And bloom again where you repose.
Exude your fragrance, like a rose.

We were the buds upon your tree.
You tended us so wistfully
With love encased in mystery—
Pre-occupied with destiny.

Somehow you cleared the way for us
To dream and work with little fuss,
To greet each day with hope anew.
We heard you sing. That's how we grew.

THERE'S NO FAMILY
LIKE MINE

There's no father like my father
There's no mother like my mother
There's no sister like my sister—
There's no family like mine.

My father sings and the door to heaven opens.
His prayers have wings—there's 'kavanah' in his motions.
Since he retired, he's had two homes,
And one of them's the 'shul.'
He davvens once, he davvens twice
And then he davvens 'noch a mool'!

There's no father like my father
There's no mother like my mother
There's no sister like my sister—
There's no family like mine.

My mother keeps up with the latest in nutrition
Because she cares about the human condition.
If the doctor mentions surgery,
She gets not one opinion,
But two or three, and then, you see,
She uses her own remedy!

There's no mother like my mother
There's no father like my father
There's no sister like my sister—
There's no family like mine.

My sister writes with the flair of the artistic.
She shapes a world you imagine realistic.
She'd never stoop to compromise—the pressures notwithstanding—
The quality of what she writes
To avert misunderstanding!

> There's no sister like my sister
> There's no mother like my mother
> There's no father like my father
> There's no family like mine—oh, no—
> There's no family like mine!!!

Carolyn Luger Vermes

PORTRAIT OF YOU

When you were born, there should have been an earthly quiver
To herald the start, not the end.
Like a new stream branched off from a river—
A sudden release to shatter false peace—
Why pretend?

Deep in your eyes I saw the cares not yet forgotten
That made you tender, yet strong.
You banished the night and brought in the light
When you sang me your song.

> I, too, had fears
> Of losing the past and using up my years.
> But, then, out of the blue
> You came along to help me make it through.

Now, though you're gone, your portrait stirs my recollection—
Proof of what life could deliver—
A look so refined, a critical mind,
And the heart—the heart of a giver.

BELATED FRIENDSHIP
(If We Had Met When We Were Young)

If we had met when we were young,
The best of friends we'd have become,
Exploring worlds of earth and sky
Like little tomboys, you and I,
And sharing dolls and books and clothes
In quiet moments of repose.

If we had met when we were young
About the good things we'd have sung,
Revealing truth in simple things—
Dancing, for the joy it brings,
Playing 'til the changing light
Would draw a curtain for the night.

And we'd remember risking flight
In an imaginary plight
As to the winds we would have flung
Ourselves to soar, though we'd have clung
To one another in the fear
We'd lose each other in the dare.

Was it not destined long ago
That we should meet?—But who could know
That starting at this place and time—
The innocence of youth, behind—
We'd strike a friendship casually
Meant to endure eternally?

I HEAR YOUR VOICE

I hear your voice in the rippling of the water.
I hear your voice in the rustling of the leaves.
You mustn't say that I'll hear your voice no longer—
That is not what my heart believes.

You came to me when you needed reassuring.
I told you then that to force it would be wrong.
"Just whistle softly and give your voice a rest,
And you'll be singing, before long."

    I heard you whistling softly.
    I heard you crying softly.
    I know you tried to sing your song.

    THINGS TAKE TIME . . .
    STOP FEELING SORRY FOR YOURSELF
    AND YOU WILL FIND . . .
    YOU'LL LEARN A LOT ABOUT YOURSELF

I've never seen any ripples on the water.
I've never seen how the autumn paints the leaves.
But I can feel all the anguish in your voice
When you try singing loud and long.

    You've got me whistling softly.
    You've got me crying softly.
    I need to hear you sing your song.
    I need to hear you sing your song!

WE ARE ALWAYS WAITING, PAPA

One day you asked your little boy,
"What would you like to be?"
I said, "A daddy just like you
Who roams the land and sea."
I show my friends your letters
And they know the tales are true.
You're not only my hero
But you're their hero, too.

> We are always waiting, Papa
> Waiting for your return.
> I can see on Mama's face
> The longing, the concern.
> Must you stay away so long?
> It really isn't fair
> When you know your family's waiting here.

One day you asked your growing boy,
"What would you like to do?"
I said that, more than anything,
I'd like to be with you.
And when the new moon rises
Over Istanbul,
We could watch together
Until the moon waxed full.

> (Refrain)

One day I felt like bringing
My own father to his knees.
I thought of how we'd suffered

While he did as he damn-well pleased.
Answering to no one—
Just the impulse of his mind—
Leaving, without conscience,
His family behind.

(Refrain)

I left to stay with Father
For a time in Istanbul.
We talked the talk of grown-up men
And watched the moon grow full.
But he was just as far from me
As if I were back home.
He could be contented
Where I'd feel so alone.

(Refrain)

The day he died, I felt the pain,
It's etched upon my face.
He'd left me as he always had
For some exotic place.
But this time it was different—
When I settled his affairs,
I found he'd saved my letters—
In his own way, Papa cared!

(Hum Refrain)

. . . Must you stay away so long?
It really isn't fair
When you know your family is waiting here.

ARIZONA

Don't you cry, little friend, don't you cry.
I'll be back from Arizona, by and by.
As a friend, you ought to know
That no matter where I go,
There's no end, round the bend—
No goodbye.

We had fun times together for a while.
When I think what we've been through,
I have to smile.
And though miles are placed between us,
Anyone who's ever seen us, would say
When we meet, we'll do it up in style!

Wipe your eyes, little friend, wipe your eyes
Or you'll flood the sands and spoil my turquoise skies.
Wipe your eyes . . .

I'M YOUR FRIEND

Call, if you need me.
You should know that I care.
All I can offer
I would happily share.
You just have to ask me,
And I'll come to your side.
There's no real place
For a runner to hide;
So, remember, when you reach a 'dead end,'
I'm your friend.

Life isn't hollow
If you fill it with love.
Let your eye follow
The flight of a dove.
But if you should falter,
As everyone does,
You can always
Give me a buzz.
Just remember, I'm for real, not pretend
I'm your friend.

LIFE WITHOUT FRIENDSHIP
IS LIKE A LOCK WITHOUT A KEY. I'M SO
VERY THANKFUL
THAT I FOUND YOU AND YOU FOUND ME.

For, working together is a wonderful thing,
Whether we're crying or trying to sing.
And, if there's a problem,
Why suffer alone?
They say, 'Two heads
Are better than one.'
I'll stand by you,
You can bet, 'til the End.
I'm your friend.

Carolyn Luger Vermes

YOU ARE YOUR BROTHER'S KEEPER

Gonna write a song for Abel,
Gonna write a song for Cain.
Won't resort to any labels
So neither party stands to gain.
'Cause in the past there's been some trouble,
So now I'm gonna make it plain . . .

> YOU ARE YOUR BROTHER'S KEEPER,
> IF THERE'S EVER BEEN A DOUBT,
> AND THE NEED FOR LOVE GOES DEEPER
> THAN YOU'VE EVER BEEN ABLE TO FIGURE OUT.

Now, it's Ish-ma-el and Isaac—
The past is surfacing once more,
Threat-en-ing to blow the cover,
So no one's left to keep the score.
Why not agree that you are brothers—
Not rivals, as you were before? . . .

> YOU ARE YOUR BROTHER'S KEEPER,
> IF THERE'S EVER BEEN A DOUBT,
> AND THE NEED FOR LOVE GOES DEEPER
> THAN YOU'VE EVER BEEN ABLE TO FIGURE OUT.

So, try to get along together.
It will serve you well, my friends.
The winds of change may bring rough weather.
On you the world may well depend.
So, why not change the path you've taken?
Peace is just around the bend . . .

(Hum Chorus to fade out.)

REFLECTIONS
PHILOSOPHICAL

BREATH OF LIFE

I draw breath of Life

and breathe out

my own . . .

I JUST CAME TO PLAY MY SONG

Well, I sat down to dine with these friends of mine.
It wasn't the pie, and it wasn't the wine—
I felt fine . . .
But I just came to play my song.

"Have some fish chowder—it's a shame to waste.
Watch out for the bones; you can season to taste."
I know it's wrong . . .
But I just came to play my song.

Well, now, friends of the fam'ly were speaking in French.
I'm watching the action from the piano bench.
I'm still strong . . .
On playing my song.

No, I don't need food of the regular kind.
Food for the soul helps the body and mind
To stay young . . .
So, I just came to play my song.

I keep a melody inside my head
So, while the world is bickering,
I'm hearing music, instead.

Yes, I played my guitar, and I hadn't got far
When the smiles all around stopped the rain coming down!
Well, so long!
I just came to play my song.
I feel I belong when I get to play my song,
When I get to play my song . . .
I got to play my song!

Carolyn Luger Vermes

EVERY MORNING IS A
NEW BEGINNING

Every morning is a new beginning.
Every step you take can point a new way.
So, stop complaining—I don't care if it is raining—
'Cause nothing can put a damper on my day.

Wake up, brothers, don't be Rip Van Winkles.
Wake up, brothers, you've been sleeping too long.
The air is changing, and a toast we'll be exchanging
If we can still distinguish right from wrong.

So, let us sing, and call the stranger, "Brother."
Though we're different, let's still accept each other,
And the mornings will be that much brighter
And our step a little bit lighter.

SIGNS OF THE SEASON

Windows blind with glacial mist,
An elastic shopping list,
Voices that from choirs rise,
A newly-fallen snow surprise;
Cards that over-simplify
What to each other we deny.
Love and kindness for a while,
Followed by the fading smile.

TIME OUT

A time to reflect, away from commotion,
On life, as we're living it, year after year:
Predictable crises—replete with emotion—
Trying the patience of those we hold dear.
A time for new goals, new journeys and places
A change from the past, inevitably.
No longer slaves to habitual races—
Exploring whoever we happen to be.

NEGANTICIPATION

Describe the wind as 'blustery'
And you will feel the cold.
Consider challenge harmful
And disaster is foretold.

That's not to say be mindless
Of the dangers all around,
But what of all the love and beauty
Waiting to be found?

Carolyn Luger Vermes

WINTER PERSPECTIVES

The cold breath of winter revives, so we find,
Scenes of the past never lost in the mind:
Of gliding down slopes, with your body pressed tight
Against the wood slats, feeling lighter than light—
A freedom to match that of gulls in their flight—
A statement of being, denying the fright.
Again, thoughts are working to set things aright—
To blot out the darkness and cover it white.

LOVE IS LIKE A CAROUSEL

Love is like a carousel,
Spinning you around until you think you've left the ground,
But can you tell?
How is one to know that it is real and not a show?
When your heart desires, can one say, "No!"?

I have seen such love descend
From dizzying, passionate flights
To tears in the end.
How tempting is love
That's like the summer skies—
A glorious diamond display
For blinding two eyes!

LOVE—how like a carousel,
Spinning you around until you think you're slowing down . . .
It's just as well.

CRYCYCLE

From crisis to crisis. we seemingly go
Without pause to ponder just why it is so.
Perhaps in our haste we've neglected to strive
For what would give meaning to 'Being Alive!'

RENEWAL FEVER

(For a New Millenium)

It's going around . . . renewal fever,
It makes you want to improve on the past.
It's easy to catch . . . renewal fever.
You can look forward to something, at last!

> Refrain:
>> In your thoughts and in your dreams,
>> In waking visions and private screams,
>> There's a voice coming through—
>> It's your soul calling you.

There is no cure for this kind of fever.
Good things will happen if you stay the course.
Move toward the Light—become a believer.
The wave of the future is back to the Source.

> (Refrain)

Imagine the world in one celebration!
Where would you be, and what would you do?
Would there be some great revelation?
Would the predictions really come true?

> (Refrain)

It's going around . . .
It's going around . . .
It's going around . . .
Catch it!

Carolyn Luger Vermes

TRUTH

Aiming down
>   through moving noise and organized
>   distraction,
>   it settles
>   in quiet, hidden
>   places of mind,

Harboring
>   the seed of knowledge
>   that topples
>   false gods.

MY CREDO

I will choose to live life anew every day.
I will choose to make my own way
In a world where people don't do as they say.
I will choose to live, anyway.

I will choose to work for the good that I see.
In this world, we're all family.
In my heart I know that what peace there may be
Comes to those who live honestly.

    I never realized the power I possess
    To bring about a state of true happiness.
    I was too busy earning what gave me less
    Until—suddenly—I confronted me.

I will find somebody to share in my dreams
Who will work in peace at my side,
And when time runs out and life ends, so it seems,
Then at least I'll know that I tried.
Yes, at least I'll know that I tried.

MY LIFE 'TIL NOW

My life 'til now has been without a friendship that could comfort me
On days when I don't recognize myself as me—
The scornful days, the mournful days.

My life 'til now has been a preparation for a time ahead
When I can lead, instead of always being led.
I'll take it slow, until I know

> That I'm ready for the changes that will come.
> And I won't pin my hopes on anything or anyone.
> So, if you choose to take me as I am,
> You're in my plan.

My life 'til now might not make a movie or a TV show,
But it has taught me what I really need to know:
To find a role that suits my soul.

So, if you care, you'll join me on a journey to a place somewhere,
Where we could make a difference in the life that's there.
We'll take it slow, until we know

> That we're ready for the changes that will come,
> And we won't pin our hopes on anything or anyone.
> And though things may not always go our way,
> We'll be O.K.

My life 'til now has seen the best and worst
of what this world can be.
It's meaning? As elusive as its destiny
That few can know, from here, below.

Why do I feel the anguish of a people half a world away,
Not knowing whether it's enough to weep and pray?
That's when I think I hear G-d say

      That He'll guide us through the changes that will come
      And not to pin our hopes on anything or anyone,
      And though it hasn't always been sublime,
      My life 'til now has not been wasted time.

RIVER OF LOVE

Wake the river of love
    and it will caress you
        with every ebb and flow.

Arouse it further
    and be engulfed.

FLAME OF LIFE

Like a flame that soars
and then succumbs,
must I go out—
my last chance
at this
firedance?

THE TIMES OF MAN

When times are "bad,"
Man stands in judgment of himself—
   the pain he thinks he caused,
     the things he failed to do.

When times are "good,"
Man is too busy to remember
     the hands that buoyed him up
     (that now would anchor him.)

In times "uncertain,"
Man stands on shaky ground.
The beating of his heart replaces time,
And in the pause that follows—
     sometimes final, sometimes not—
Man learns the truth about himself.

LET US ALL STRIVE
TO BE HAPPY

I lie awake and wonder
What my life will be
Twenty years from here and now—
A small eternity.

Will we be together?
Will we realize
Some of the dreams that always seem
To shine from youthful eyes?

LET US ALL STRIVE TO BE HAPPY
LET'S NOT HAVE ONE FALSE REGRET
LET US TAKE ON EVERY BURDEN
LIKE A CHALLENGE TO BE MET.
DON'T BE TRAPPED BY FEAR OF LOSING.
NEVER LOVING LEAVES A VOID.
LET'S JUST RISE ABOVE THIS PETTY WORLD.
THEN OUR FAITH CAN'T BE DESTROYED.

I often see around me
How fortunes rise and fall.
There may come a time when they lose their last dime,
And they don't want to live at all.
Well, I tell them life's worth living,
That they must take control
And do what they can, with G-d in their plan
To re-define their goal.

LET US ALL STRIVE TO BE HAPPY
LET'S NOT HAVE ONE FALSE REGRET
LET US TAKE ON EVERY BURDEN
LIKE A CHALLENGE TO BE MET.
DON'T BE TRAPPED BY FEAR OF FAILING,
NEVER TRYING LEAVES A VOID.
LET'S JUST RISE ABOVE THIS PETTY WORLD.
THEN OUR FAITH CAN'T BE DESTROYED.

Sometimes I can't hack it.
The blood runs from my head.
I need to keep my body
From thinking it is dead.
But then the answer comes to me.
I pray with shallow breath.
And somehow I know it's not the last show—
There's more to life than death!

LET US ALL STRIVE TO BE HAPPY
LET'S NOT HAVE ONE FALSE REGRET
LET US TAKE ON EVERY BURDEN
LIKE A CHALLENGE TO BE MET.
DON'T BE TRAPPED BY FEAR OF DYING—
LIFE IS YET TO BE ENJOYED!
LET'S JUST RISE ABOVE THIS PETTY WORLD.
THEN OUR FAITH CAN'T BE DESTROYED!

TONIGHT I LOST A PRECIOUS THING

Tonight I lost a precious thing—
A love that moved the heart to sing,
Who brought a joy to everything in life.

Tonight I'll face the world alone,
And all the treasures that I own
Might just as well be made of stone, tonight.

Why did my life take this turn?
Is there some lesson to learn?
Once there was such happiness.
Must I be thankful for less?

Dear G-d, I'll bend my will to Yours
If that is what will open doors.
You've shown me how a soul endures, tonight.
Pray show me that the soul you freed
From earthly pain and misery
Is somewhere living happily, tonight.

Carolyn Luger Vermes

FROM YOU TO YOU

Give yourself a present,
Make yourself feel good,
Especially when plans
Are not progressing as they should.

Think of starting over,
Seeing things anew—
All the joys you missed before
That life holds out to you.

COMFORT

As a breeze might waft me upward
Were I light enough to fly,
So your smile could send me sunward
From the gloom in which I lie.

Just your presence is a comfort,
Faking sunshine (still a balm),
Soothing tensions of estrangement
Like the words of David's psalm.

THERE'S STILL TIME

How many times have I walked this way,
Kicking up dust aimlessly?
I claimed tomorrow but lost today.
Now, I'm not where I want to be.

BUT THERE'S STILL TIME . . .
AS LONG AS LIFE GOES ON.
THERE'S STILL TIME TO SET IT STRAIGHT.
THERE'S STILL TIME . . .
THOUGH MANY A CHANCE IS GONE,
IT'S NOT TOO LATE.
THERE'S STILL TIME . . .

How many times have I felt despair,
Knowing my motives were vain?
I never showed people that I cared.
Now I am feeling the pain.

(Refrain)

How many times have I said a prayer,
Seeking the blessing of peace?
Bottled-up feelings too deep to share
Wait for their day of release.

BUT, THERE'S STILL TIME . . .
AS LONG AS LIFE GOES ON.
THERE'S STILL TIME TO SET IT STRAIGHT.
THERE'S STILL TIME . . .
THOUGH MANY A CHANCE IS GONE.
IT'S NOT TOO LATE.
THERE'S STILL TIME . . .

I'M NO LOSER

I'm no loser,
But that's what some people would say.
I don't choose to
Be part of the game that they play.

It's not easy
To stand up for what you believe in
When the one that you care for is leavin'
And the years of your youth slip away.

     But, I'm no loser,
     I'm no loser.
     Yes, it's somethin' I've learned:
     Don't let getting burned keep you down.

     No, I'm no loser,
     I'm no loser.
     When the time's right,
     I know I'll be comin' around.

I'm no loser
'Cause I've got a life left to live.
There's no user
Who can use up the love I can give.

When the blow comes

To any affair,
Disillusion can bring to the heart such confusion
That you almost give up in despair.

   But, I'm no loser,
   I'm no loser.
   Yes, it's somethin' I've learned:
   Don't let getting burned keep you down.

   No, I'm no loser,
   I'm no loser.
   When the time's right,
   I know I'll be comin' around.

CHOOSE LIFE

Choose life . . .
Through pain and sorrow.
Choose life,
There's still tomorrow.
It's G-d's gift to you.
If you follow through,
There's much more to do . . .

Choose life . . .
The bittersweet music
That's life.
We all abuse it
And that takes its toll.
But with the right goal,
We can gain control . . .

> At night,
> When you're awakened by fright,
> Don't let it shake your belief in yourself.
> Don't punish yourself—
> Just do what is right.

In your life . . .
Think of who needs you.
Choose life.
Go where life leads you.
We're meant to be here,
Though why isn't clear,
And time is so dear.
Choose life . . . choose life.
Choose life . . . CHOOSE LIFE!

THE SCHOOL OF HARD KNOCKS

"Why is life so hard?" we ask,
As we sigh with each new task.
What might Shakespeare have to say?
"Get thee out of thine own way!"

CONFIDENCE

With half a gut
one can strut
over any rut.

HAPPY ENDINGS

All endings are really beginnings.
The 'happy' part is ours to create.

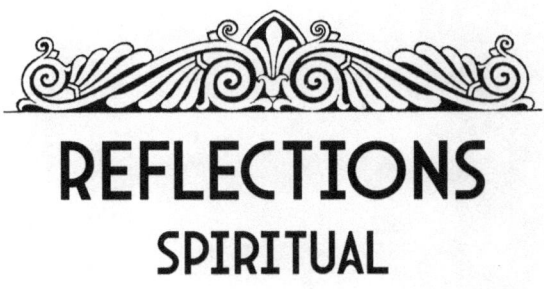

REFLECTIONS
SPIRITUAL

GUARD THY TONGUE

Guard thy tongue,
Don't let it slip.
It just won't do
To 'shoot from the hip.'

Be diplomatic
For the sake of peace.
Restrain your inner tiger—
Find some other release.

There's strength in restraint.
Turn to song, books, or paint
Before you alarm
And cause someone harm.

Beneath the agitation,
There's a cry for validation.
But, if that probes too deep,
Just remember when you speak:

Guard thy tongue—
It's a blessing on loan—
And the life you save
May be your own!

INNER LIGHT

Where is love, that I may feel it?
Where is faith, that I may know
There is hope, that I may lay it
At the feet of those brought low?

"Call upon your inner vision,"
Comes a voice to answer me.
"In the darkest part of living
There is Light by which we see."

CAN IT BE?

Can it be . . . there is Someone who's all-knowing,
Leading me on the path on which I'm going,
By a still, small voice,
Yet leaving room for choice?

Can it be there's a reason for believing?
Would I know it's the truth that I'm receiving?
What if there should be A Power who cares for me!

> Can it be, in a world so filled with woe,
> That destiny is a friend and not a foe?
> Let us know . . .

That it can be, if the good is what we're stressing
And what we do is designed to bring a blessing,
That we may come to see
A time of peace, a time of harmony.

> Oh, can it be, can it be
> That one day we all will know why
> We love and we work to get by,
> We live and we die?
> Why?

Can it be . . . it's a good thing to be needing
Someone who takes delight in my succeeding—
Someone who can see the noblest part of me?

Oh, can it be, in a world so filled with woe,
That destiny is a friend and not a foe?
Let us know . . .

That it can be, if the good is what we're stressing
And what we do is designed to bring a blessing,
That we may come to see
A time of peace, a time of harmony—
Let it be! Let it be! Let it be!!!

THE LADDER

He who climbs a ladder
And then begins to fall
Might think, "How foolish
To have even climbed at all."

But, if he knew the ladder led
To where the soul finds peace,
The drive to master every rung
Would notably increase.

MESSIAH

When life is reduced to the trivial,
When feelings are programmed out,
When values default, through expedience,
Belief giving way to doubt,
Who will come forward to teach us
That this is the way to the End?
Who will bring light to the darkness
To heal every heart that would mend?

FORBIDDEN FRUIT
(Paradise Lost)

Serpent: "It will not hurt you.
I would alert you
If there were danger.
I am no stranger.
You surely will not die—
You might get 'high'"

Eve: "But Adam told me
What G-d had told him—
Not to be hasty
Though it be tasty—
Not to touch or eat of that tree,
Or woe is me!"

THEN THE SERPENT PUSHED HER TOWARD THE TREE,
RE-ASSURING HER, SEDUCTIVELY
IN A VOICE THAT SOUNDED HEAVENLY,
BUT UNDERNEATH THE SWEET VENEER—
AN EVIL SNEER!

Eve: "Why did he tell me
That G-d had told him
Not to be hasty
Though it be tasty?

Now that I've touched the tree—
I am still me!"

Serpent: "Bite the fruit—peel it!
Let your tongue feel it,
Layer by layer,"
Coaxed the betrayer.
But underneath his breath,
A whisper of death . . .

NOW THE WOMAN SAW WITH OPENED EYES
THINGS SHE'D NEVER SEEN IN PARADISE.
SHE GAVE THE FRUIT TO ADAM, AND HE ATE!
NOW WE, TODAY, CANNOT ESCAPE THEIR FATE . . .

G: "Adam, where are you?
This is G-d calling.
Why are you hiding?
Why are you crawling?"

Adam: "I ate the fruit of that tree—
She gave it to me."

G: "Eve, what's your story?"

Eve: "There's not much to it.
The serpent deceived me—
He made me do it!"

G: "Now, I must punish all three, Unhappily . . .

ADAM, YOU WILL TOIL AND YOU WILL SWEAT!
THE EARTH WILL GIVE FORTH MORE THAN YOU WILL GET.
WOMAN, YOU WILL BEAR YOUR CHILD IN PAIN—
AND, AFTERWARDS, YOU'LL CRAVE YOUR MAN, AGAIN.

> Serpent of evil,
> You have succeeded.
> You have uprooted
> What I have seeded.
>> On your belly, you'll crawl—
>> The lowest of all!

> As for the woman,
> She will despise you.
> You will be stepped on—
> She won't recognize you.

> For betraying her trust,
> You shall eat dust!"

> "Garden of Eden . . .

Adam & Eve: Farewell!"

Carolyn Luger Vermes

"TREE OF LIFE"

Honors hang, inscribed on "leaves"
Upon a "Tree of Life,"
Reminders of the kinship
Between success and strife.
But, greater than the feats of men
Who claim life as their own
Are the efforts of the humble
To make ripe what G-d has sown.

CHILDREN OF THE LIGHT

Children of the Light,
Have you lost your way?
Speak to Me with words of truth.
I'll hear what you say.

    Where are you going?
    "To our homeland."
    And what will you do?
    "We will pray."
    And what are you after?
    Is it closeness to your God?
    Then, go in peace, and may you find your way.

Soon your tears will fall,
Watering the ground,
Where the holy lie in peace,
Speaking, without sound.

    Where are you going?
    "To our homeland."
    And what will you do?
    "We will pray."
    And what are you after?
    Is it justice for us all?
    Then, go in peace, and may you find your way.

IT IS A JOURNEY THAT DOESN'T END.
YOU OCCUPY A SPACE FOR A TIME.
YOU GROW IN WISDOM, YOU LEARN WHEN TO
BEND.
THROUGH THE LOVE OF G-D, YOU TASTE THE
SUBLIME!

Children of the Light,
Where are you today?
Do for me your deeds of love.
They will light your way.

Where are you going?
"To our homeland."
And what will you do?
"We will pray."
And what are you after?
"G-d's forgiveness, for us all,
And we'll keep working at it every day!"

Be sure you're working at it every day,
Children of the Light!

MOVIN' ON

Movin' out of the city,
Far from the crowds . . .
Gonna set my sights on a mountain,
And give my mind a free ride among the clouds.

Refrain: I'm movin' on, movin' on.
   Gonna find me a place before I'm gone.
   I'm movin' on, movin' on.
   Gonna find the place where I belong.

Movin' into the suburbs,
What do I find?
Sin is making lots more conversions
Than all of the religions on earth combined!

  So, I'm . . . (Refrain)

Movin' on to fulfillment,
Morally strong . . .
Though the road is paved with illusion,
And my only weapons are prayer and song.

   Yes, I'm movin' on, movin' on.
   Gonna find me a place before I'm gone.
   I'm movin' on, movin' on.
   Gonna find a place, before too long.

IN PRAISE OF THEE

I love Thee with the innocence of a child.
I love Thee with a song that's pure, undefiled.
I see in You what I had hoped would be.
I see in You my true destiny.

I love Thee for the love you bring to my heart.
I love Thee for the wisdom you impart.
My body cleaves to ways that set us apart.
My mind perceives not what Thou truly art.

How far we should see,
Were our bodies free—
Slave to only Thee,
Craving only Thee!

I love Thee for the beauty You inspire.
I love Thee for the duty You require.
My lips express what my soul knows as true:
Blessed be the name that is You!

TRIBUTE

BLOOM WHERE YOU ARE PLANTED

"Bloom where you are planted."
So the adage goes.
Why here, not there?
Why now, not then?
There's reason, do you suppose?

Carolyn Luger Vermes

NEW JERSEY,
WE SALUTE YOU!

New Jersey, with true admiration
We stand, to salute you today,
And we sing, in celebration,
Of the role in our lives that you play.

> You are known, Garden State, for your beauty
> That we hope to preserve for all time.
> We've the priv'lege, also the duty,
> To say, "I am proud this is mine."

New Jersey, we'll not take for granted
The treasures we have here at hand:
The parks, lakes, the rivers, the Ocean,
The Shore, where the sun warms the sand.

> The tall trees that tower above you,
> The fruit of the earth that is grown,
> Though silent, they speak volumes of you
> In languages all their own.

New Jersey, with due recognition
We stand, to salute you today.
You've earned, beyond wealth and position,
The praise that is coming your way:

You have courage for bold innovation,
The wisdom to learn and to grow
With values that founded our nation.
Yes, this is the Jersey we know.

New Jersey, with firm resolution
We stand, to salute you today.
Your laws and your fine constitution
We pledge to uphold, come what may.

May God bless our state and its people
With leaders both worthy and true,
Who will merit respect and allegiance
From the many as well as the few.

New Jersey, with true inspiration
We stand, to salute you today.
You rank with the best in the nation—
That calls for a rousing "Hooray!"

New Jersey, we salute you today!

This song was a submission to a New Jersey State Competition

I often dream that words convey
What I really mean to say.
If words were more like food, well-chewed,
I would be better understood.

ABOUT THE AUTHOR

Born in the Bronx, Carolyn Luger Vermes holds a B.A. degree from New York University and an M.A. degree from Yeshiva University. She taught mathematics in the Westchester School System and studied voice with Mme. Herta Sperber in Manhattan until the birth of her first son.

Carolyn has drawn inspiration for her lyrics from the impactful experiences of family, friends, co-workers, persons in the news, as well as from spiritual concepts and her own imagination. Her melodies come from somewhere, within.

She currently resides in New York State, where she continues to produce her uplifting words and music. You can hear her songs at www.Lugerland Arts.com and at www.RadioAirplay.com. She also can be heard (as Carolyn Luger) on YouTube.